Trace

TRACE

SIMONE MUENCH

Black
Lawrence
Press

Black
Lawrence
Press

www.blacklawrence.com

Executive Editor: Diane Goettel
Chapbook Editor: Kit Frick
Book Layout: Amy Freels
Cover Design: Richard Every
Cover Art: *The Scribe* by Robert and Shana ParkeHarrison. Used with permission.

Black Lawrence Press
326 Bigham Street
Pittsburgh, PA 15211

Published 2014 by Black Lawrence Press.
Printed in the United States.

Hence, my writing is, if not a cabinet of fossils,
a kind of collection of flies in amber.
—Marianne Moore

Contents

With flowers in their lapels, nine

howling wolves come hungering.

A surge of wet syllables

dangles from their mouths.

Children trace their liquid howl

built out of alien words like seeds

in black earth. A woman's lock

of hair brushes their lips.

Their jaws open—coral

in the darkness. I do not know

who has opened the window.

They sing with their mouths full of earth.

The light is putting on gloves.

No blood is flowing. Just red birds.

Wolf Cento

Outside the new world winters in grand dark
like a young wolf in its blood leaping
to snap the flower-flake as my shadow
falls broken-legged down stony precipices,
snowflakes falling more blue than subways,
than astronomy—the body-clocks are stopped
all over town. Your finger drawing my mouth.
Sans teeth, sans eyes.

When the mouth dies, who misses you?
The kill of the wolf is the meat of the wolf:
he may do what he will.
Inside the wolf's tongue, the doe's tears.
It was wet & we licked the hollow
where a hare could hide.

Wolf Cento

Who will take the madness from the trees?
The petals of dead planets broken.
What do they matter now, the deprivations.

Your voice will never recover
what was said once, so when you hold
the hemisphere & once more take up the world,

I can see myself in you as though I were sitting
in a beautiful wound. I drink from your footprint
& see: a red wolf strangled by an angel

against the immeasurable sun. This terrifying
world is not devoid of charms—
the poppy that no girl's finger has opened,

farmhouses dark against a sublime blue,
an airplane whistling from the other world.
In the distance someone is singing. In the distance

a slow, sweet song crowded with floating animals

& small artifacts: bell jar, honeycomb, revolver.

Can we describe the world this way—

with stars & bullet holes? A presence or its contrary?

Like dizzy horses that dissolve into a dust of sheen,

I pass through them as they pass through me.

Wolf Cento

Very quick. Very intense, like a wolf

at a live heart, the sun breaks down.

What is important is to avoid

the time allotted for disavowals

as the livid wound

leaves a trace   leaves an abscess

takes its contraction for those clouds

that dip thunder & vanish

like rose leaves in closed jars.

Age approaches, slowly. But it cannot

crystal bone into thin air.

The small hours open their wounds for me.

This is a woman's confession:

I keep this wolf because the wilderness gave it to me.

Wolf Cento

Sea-blue, shot through
with the echo of a shadow
that sleeps after its voyage,

she sat with wolves & magicians
in a corner of an empty house
& saw someone coming

through the whirling snow
like a reflection from arson,
emitting sparks, shaking

the air as if to remind her
of the animal life.
A word, a whisper says this

in the dark: you are feverishly hot.
Forest stands behind forest.
Under your skins you have

other skins; you have a seventh
sense. Don't you hear
the sky ping above your eye?

All of us are rain
under rain, noon spin
through bright meridian.

Mind drawn on, drawn out
like a little boat bringing
the flame from the other shore.

Wolf Cento

I have looked too long into human eyes.
I have stood for a long time
like a dream printed on paper
while all the leaves leaked gold
as the wolf sang once again—
nerve-sprung & half electric
in the dark tree of the self.
You will always be at some border
of a blue blade: a lunar
landscape of wounds; a river net
of anatomy. Your animal companion.
Show them the marks left where you merged.

Wolf Cento

I watch my life running away
with a wolf's speed. I want to stop
this desolation, like tiny cities,
a long, dark, sad tongue.

Here the air smells like crime.
Come, be my camera.
Let me have an indecent dream.
Don't let me become the last fly
with his eyes made of glass,
wandering from one body to ash.

I'll take whatever breaks down
beneath its own sad weight—
felled trees in broken speech,
the ravaged sclerotic hearts
of animals perishing, houses burning.

What is ruined rises up
with dark blue pebbles & heliotropes.

A dying animal now wakes among the ruins

like the outline of a sunlit room

whose only guest is the branches of a peach.

Wolf Cento

It was a desire rather than a boat
ruffling the gasoline moons in the harbor
as it climbed over centuries & bones
& held the breath of the naked.
With wolftrap eyes, your flesh
remembers our secret
kept so well & so badly.
To damage is an animal hunch
& urge at the approach of a mouth
murmuring a hidden name. What beast
of saliva & suet has moistened my bones?
A flame, an inverted tear circling our bodies
always in the open field—acidic music
of thistles. Don't burn if I kiss someone else.
Eros is a wolf, Caesar.
Through the thickets your paws break.

There are wolves in the next room

waiting when I turn towards you

snake-spined, all Pentecostal shivers

beneath the sun's cooled carbon wing

as we wait for something which is not the rain.

Step by step you leave yourself—

the ship of a clear October's end.

Our lives are language, our desire apophatic:

the stars slowly clicking themselves apart

like bees that forget the topography of their hives.

Now that all your distance surrounds me,

your mouth is the blue door I walk through.

Its bright impossibility pours into me & vanishes

in those stars whose light speaks a language.

The beautiful boys will run in that light

where honey tightens in a coherence of rays

where my sleepwalker's movements slide

like rain running under the peach tree,

sweet vowels of shadow & water.

The world has only one voice.

It's not you I've lost.

Wolf Cento

How long have I left you?—played the wolf
or the witch. There I was without a face,

where the river freezing & fabled condenses
to a point, stalled in forgetfulness & salt.

In my ear, the tongue of a stranger.
That's the way it goes in the dark. One card,

one turn: two dogs bark at the moon,
kept awake by the same laws.

We saw the wounds of our country
appear on our skins. An entire

butcher's woods hemmed your bare neck
with a red band of mist, an orange wash

in which every edge frays—
all else is the shade of alien wildwood.

There's a soft spot in everything,

a hollow place where no one goes;

a door I've closed until the end of the world.

Let the wind come, let my house burn.

I'll spread my thin arms to hide the fire.

Regardless of how perishable we are, here,

I dwell in your ear: the hull of a dream,

black against the coastline's pink.

Wolf Cento

In moon-swallowed shadows
amid the tiger-purring greenery
I take a wolf's rib & whittle it
into little months, little smokes
& oblivion. Beautiful,
those boys among the roses
where fiery blossoms clot the light
& we lick the blood off our paws.
How many have died
in sweeter morgues?
It was all like a childhood picture:
our windows ravenous
as snow wolves & again
a rose-petal falls in an empty bed.

Wolf Cento

I saw my life a wolf loping along the road—

a glint of bone, visible & then gone,

a landscape altered.

Ideas, hair, fingers

fall & come to naught.

A shirt blows across the field.

A shrug of stars as flowers go out on the sea.

Maybe the whole world is absentminded

or floating. The flower, the weather,

the room empties its mind of me,

the sea-pulse of my utterance.

I have stood for a long time

at the edge of a river, unknown, nameless,

hands groping for the shape of the animal.

Not knowing what all the music had been hiding.

Wolf Cento

When tenderness seems tired,

the girl nestles down in me

with her she-wolf's mask,

places a word in the hollow

of my mute being.

Impossible to be alone

in language, light of bird-

laden lemon trees.

We're between blue & good evening,

heaving with brilliants: the mortal

glitter of the naked beach,

the glass horizon.

(It is the human that is alien.)

Even with her severed tongue

the she-wolf bathes herself

in the blue vertigo in my mouth

where the planets flicker.

The orange tree breaks into foam

& no god comes.

November stands at the door.

Tonight, the wolf is a solitary shadow

that spills between stone & revery

as bodies resume their boundaries.

Through open French windows

the forest edge enfolds blue animals

& behind the trees, the river—

its strange nakedness of wide

solitary margins. What have I known

but its bending? No more

second self, nor changing face,

no more wild lament of broken

mouths, red clouds. Scarcely

more than a word with no echo,

little tracks in the snow. Facedown,

I lick away the footprints.

Nothing remains of you. The city

rotates in the canal's fluorescence

caught between the rains of obese trees

dripping a thousand sugars

& whorls of more carnal flowers.

I go out to the road & I listen to this

fouled landscape that's sunk into itself.

Wolves yawn in front of the open cage.

Nothing glistens under the arcades.

In the parks, electric light breaks

through the branches, a man

waves from his spandex biking outfit.

Everything else is hushed

like a much-hunted animal

fixing us in her eyeshine.

We live in a world of motion & distance.

No matter where we go, we always arrive

too late & whatever houses we return to

in this stuffed masquerade,

we are at a party that doesn't love us.

Wolf Cento

Everything in these parts is geared
for winter: long dreams of falling
snow on the lead-still sea. Shadows
behind the clouded glass, exquisite
as wolf's milk. The frost
extends its immaculate forest—
a mirror by which to enter a landscape
of open eyes, a heavy fabric
in the most bull-like black.
A she-wolf, that with all hungerings,
sends a message from behind the lit woods:
you have become human, alien & hateful.
When the body is cadence of shriveled
memories, do not forget to be animal.
Someone cleans a rifle in his kitchen.
A great & royal animal is dying,
through her arms trickles black snow.
Then that chapter officially ended.
In the room where it is snowing,
I find my childhood toys.

Wolf Cento

I have lost my being in so many beings,
travelers passing by night, hard as the great wolf
who goes wounded & bleeding through the snows.

Someone has closed the door, someone
heavy with the rain of all eyes. His muzzle
has rummaged my shoulders.

Thorns illuminate. Owls swell
the shadows. The last poppy, the last
galaxy of the red dress illuminates

& scatters the opaque weight of the flesh.
That strange beneficent geography
where fingers probe the desert

of two lips, a wound where soured sugar flows,
where the landscape begins its adulthood of dust.
All is near & can't be touched.

Wolf Cento

After the first snow has fallen to its squalls,
I'll go out in the frosty dark & sing
most terribly, make a necklace
from all the rivers I have crossed
across the evening of my room.
Sing with big blue tongue,
sing until it breaks the night—
black champagne, a lamentation.

My body makes no moan but sings on
by centuries to register
the North Star, the wolf's fang
troubling me with telegrams:
my teeth are tireless.
A cloud crosses the night as the drum
reads on to the end of the thriller.
It is a light that goes out in my mouth.

Wolf Cento

All song of the woods is crushed

like crowfoot flowers in some

monstrous encyclopedia. No need

to console me: I live my life

a wind with a wolf's head.

In whatever language I would hear

the waves behind the wavelike

curtain crash, I put away my hunger.

Perhaps this music you are listening to

is lovelier than these loaned words

that have rusted green. Perhaps the green

on copper will turn into emeralds.

A landscape smokes the horizontal eloquence

of the morning starting from a frail cobweb,

vast, unstinting, flooded with transparent,

irretrievable words, a fist of nothing

driven through nothing, snowy

geometry on the animal heart.

No cause you should weep, Wolf.

Your emptiness has put on weight.

Shall I hang you on the wall,

near this window struck by rain?

Even words grow thin & transparent:

a squirrel's stretched-out skin,

empty like the cottages in fall,

whispered by one human to another.

At the instant you disappear like a splinter

in the sea, you could be a tear

in the eyes of a country. If you wish

I shall speak, not of self, but of geography.

If you wish, I shall rage on raw meat.

The wolf licks her cheeks with

       a fiery tongue—he illuminates her.

This season lasted one moment, like the pause

       between a girl's teeth

            on the edges of sleep.

How mysterious the red silence of your mouth

       —the stag throat slit by a thorn—

as you wrapped me with past

       & passing tenses, with the emptiness

            in your empty poison-tooth.

Let me tell you about yesterday:

       the first snow of your life.

It's not a horizon I see

       but a minus sign. A roof of absences

            that makes room for the silence.

All talk is barren trade.

       The future has arrived & it is not

a bullet fired from a living machine.

       It is a faint sigh lost in a vast forest.

            There is no wolf, of course—

First frost blackens with a cloven hoof;

a woman's black stocking rises like smoke

leaving the land its architecture of withdrawal.

I've heard the wolves scuffle & said:

you might as well let ugliness come.

Rosebush dead, orange trees dead.

The houses belonged to the dead.

Overgrown with reeds, the convulsive,

rheumatic shadows of men indifferent

to eating oranges. Evening descends:

a tired bird upon the smoky wet plain.

On either side of me the nights blacken,

only the track-covering slime of the fog shines.

Only a forest, perhaps, will think of me.

Ants build around the place left by my body.

The buzzard stops & becomes a star now.

Wolf Cento

You hear things. I see them.
In the forest of hours I lie back,
drain off with the sunset. This land
is my petrified rose on a rosetree
of bone. You're a long clause,
the silent wolf whose tracks
go endlessly in a straight line
in factories, in sea, on nameless islands
where I travel your body like the world.
I love your inexorable intent.

We hum, dizzy, landscape folding
the forest like an unpublishable manuscript.
Which of us is writing this page I don't know—
No history or myth has ever made us an offer
like this: the sun's last will, pomegranate,
wheat, tree flash of lake-light. We are seen
in what we see, & sweet meat.

Wolf Cento

Stunned by gold, we see coming

in full gallop, at vertiginous speed, the last sun,

frail orbits, green tries, games of stars.

We are looking for a way to live

as the she-wolf of these clouds tumbles

down through stricken dawn-dark, slanting

through the quadrant seasons, deep

between vineyards rows. With her teeth

the she-wolf reaches the blonde braid of a star,

a thing of gleaming: a radiant evanescence

the blue dogs paw.   Lick the dew

opening beautifully inside my brain

where everything is green like quetzal flowers

or the light in the skull of a bird

or a thousand tropics in an apple blossom—

What's there: the endless clear country road,

a cold drink before sunset & then a bed.

We are looking for a way to live.

Wolf Cento

I want to be strung up in a strong light & singled out,
winnowed from the water & the fire, stalked
by the she-wolf, each day to walk the wilderness
with its people, its animals, its toil & wind.

I want to unfold like Aztec hieroglyphs,
to multiply in the glass a transparent gold shirt,
exquisite as oranges & leaking muscovado casks.
To listen to the metal rattle of the world

as if there are gods somewhere
behind a vaulting sunrise, hissing salt.
A train of cranes outstretched towards alien frontiers.
I want to know there will be wine on the table.

To know the tenderness that gathers
over shoulders of wives. An open window.
A green river. The language of water.
I want everyone to know that I am still alive.

Wolf Cento

What do we leave, living?

Always the silence remains kneeling—

each letter a closed house.

& what comes after, looking back

on the mind itself, looking for home

as night drifts up like a little boat

or a pattern of small flowers.

There a screen of vertical timber,

trees fade over into fog

just as bodies flow

safe from the wolf's black jaw.

[Contain lines & fragments by the following: Anna
Akhmatova, Anne-Marie Albiach, Claribel Alegría, Dante
Alighieri, Yehuda Amichai, A. R. Ammons, Tom Andrews,
Jorge Carrera Andrade, Carlos Drummond de Andrade,
Eugenio de Andrade, Antonin Artaud, Ingeborg
Bachmann, Charles Baudelaire, Fritzi Harmsen van Beek,
Mario Benedetti, Gottfried Benn, John Berryman,
Johannes Bobrowski, Yves Bonnefoy, Jorge Luis Borges,
Coral Bracho, Kamau Brathwaite, Sophia de Mello Breyner,
Joseph Brodsky, Lucie Brock-Broido, Gwendolyn Brooks,
William Burroughs, Dino Campana, Ernesto Cardenal,
Anne Carson, Paul Celan, Aimé Césaire, Gu Cheng, Feng
Chih, John Ciardi, Alfred Corn, Jean Cocteau, Hart
Crane, Sándor Csoóri, Bei Dao, René Daumal, René
Depestre, Robert Desnos, Emily Dickinson, Ed Dorn,
Jacques Dupin, Paul Eluard, Odysseus Elytis, Faiz Ahmed
Faiz, Jean Follain, Andre Frenaud, Robert Frost, Allen
Ginsberg, Roger Giroux, Albert Goldbarth, Ángel
González, Nicolas Guillen, Eugene Guillevic, Ferreira
Gullar, Paavo Haavikko, Nazim Hikmet, Brenda Hillman,
Vladimir Holan, Miroslav Holub, Ted Hughes, Vicente
Huidobro, Sara de Ibanez, Philippe Jaccottet, Rolf Jacobsen,
Ben Jonson, Roberto Juarroz, Bhanu Kapil, Brigit Pegeen
Kelly, Galway Kinnell, Rudyard Kipling, Greta Knutson,
Edvard Kocbek, Yusef Komunyakaa, Rutger Kopland, Gerrit
Kouwenaar, Aleksei Kruchenykh, Maxine Kumin, Valery
Larbaud, Else Lasker-Schüler, Denise Levertov, Larry Levis,

Federico Garcia Lorca, Mary Low, Claire Malroux, Osip
Mandelstam, Joyce Mansour, Robert Marteau,Vladimir
Mayakovsky, Friederike Mayröcker, Cecilia Meireles, Henri
Michaux, Edna St. Vincent Millay, Czeslaw Milosz, O.V. de
L. Milosz, Gabriela Mistral, Enrique Molina, Kadya
Molodowsky, Agnes Nemes Nagy, Pablo Neruda, Joao
Cabral de Melo Neto, Henrik Nordbrandt, Ibaragi Noriko,
Charles Olson, Meret Oppenheim, Heberto Padilla,
Nicanor Parra, Pier Pasolini, Boris Pasternak, Kenneth
Patchen, Octavio Paz, Benjamin Péret, Fernando Pessoa,
Alejandra Pizarnick, Vasko Popa, Salvatore Quasimodo,
Miklos Radnoti, A.K. Ramanujan, Pierre Reverdy,
Adrienne Rich, Rainer Marie Rilke, Yannis Ritsos, Muriel
Rukeyser, Carl Sandburg, Bert Schierbeek, George Seferis,
Anne Sexton, William Shakespeare, Leonardo Sinisgalli,
Edith Sitwell, Edith Södergran, Philippe Soupault, Frank
Stafford, Wallace Stevens, Jules Supervielle, Anna Swir,
Wislawa Szymborska, Novica Tadić, Ryūichi Tamura,
Nathaniel Tarn, Allen Tate, Ha Thi Thao, Dylan Thomas,
Shu Ting, Melvin Tolson, Leo Tolstoy, Georg Trakl, Tomas
Tranströmer, Maria Tsvetaeva, Tristan Tzara, Jean
Valentine, Cesar Vallejo, Maria Elena Cruz Varela, Tomas
Venclova, Derek Walcott, Dara Wier, W. C. Williams, C.
D. Wright, Charles Wright, James Wright, W. B. Yeats,
Wen Yidou, Andrea Zanzotto]

Acknowledgments

Ample gratitude and special thanks to Gary Clark and the entire staff at Vermont Studio Center for allowing me the time, support, and a beautiful space overlooking the river to write these poems. Thanks also to the loveliness of Ray Gonzalez, Chicu Reddy, Matthea Harvey, Heather June Gibbons, and Jocelyn Casey Whiteman for providing feedback on these poems at VSC and, of course, to Kit Frick and Diane Goettel for choosing to publish *Trace*. I am deeply grateful to the Corporation of Yaddo and the National Endowment of the Arts for seeing value in this project and so generously supporting it. Finally, this manuscript would not exist without the tireless support, superlative editing skills, and continual inspiration of Jackie K. White and Hadara Bar-Nadav.

I am especially grateful to the following people who have supported, challenged, championed, and inspired me: Richard Every, Kim Ambriz, Sarah Long, Melissa Grubbs, Lana Rakhman, Virginia Smith Rice, Christine Pacyk, Catherine Blauvelt, Lanko Miyazaki, Bill Mondi, Jesse Muench, John McSween, Loretta McSween, Chuck Crowder, Clare Rothschild, Michael Anania, Sarah Gorham, Dean Rader, Jason Koo, Stephanie McCanles, Lauren Levato, Lina R. Vitkauskas, Joshua Clover, Jo Ann Beard, Tarfia Faizullah, Kim Calder, Michael Snediker, Matt Pond, Daniel Handler, Phillip Jenks, Carol Guess, and Andrew McFadyen-Ketchum.

Many thanks to the editors and staff of the following
journals for first publishing these poems:
Academy of American Poets Poem-A-Day: "Very quick. Very
   intense, like a wolf"
Another Chicago Magazine: "First frost blackens with a
   cloven hoof"
Catch Up: "Stunned by gold, we see coming" and
   "Everything in these parts is geared"
Escape Into Life: "I have lost my being in so many beings"
Fifth Wednesday Journal: "I want to be strung up in a strong
   light & singled out"
Gulf Coast: "With flowers in their lapels, nine"
The Laurel Review: "I watch my life running away,"
   "Nothing remains of you. The city," and
   "Who will take the madness from the trees?"
Mid-American Review: "No cause you should weep, Wolf."
Poets & Artists: "I have looked too long into human eyes,"
   "When tenderness seems tired," and "In moon-
   swallowed shadows"
Parthenon West Review: "After the first snow has fallen to its
   squalls," "The wolf licks her cheeks with," and "Sea-
   blue, shot through"
Pebble Lake: "November stands at the door."
Newfound Journal: "You hear things. I see them."
A Public Space: "I saw my life a wolf loping along the road"
   and "How long have I left you?—played the wolf"
Quarterly West: "What do we leave, living?," "There are
   wolves in the next room," and "It was a desire rather
   than a boat"
Salt Hill: "All song of the woods is crushed"

Whiskey Island: "Outside the new world winters in grand dark"

Thanks to Andrew McFadyen-Ketchum for anthologizing the following poems in *Apocalypse Now: Poems & Prose from the End of Days Anthology*: "Who will take the madness from the trees?," "I watch my life running away," "I have lost my being in so many beings," "The wolf licks her cheeks with," "First frost blackens with a cloven hoof," and "How long have I left you?—played the wolf."

Thanks to Jennifer Sweeney for nominating "When tenderness seems tired" for the 2011 Pushcart Prizes.

Thanks to *Verse Daily* for reprinting "With flowers in their lapels, nine."

SIMONE MUENCH is the author of *The Air Lost in Breathing* (Marianne Moore Prize; Helicon Nine, 2000), *Lampblack & Ash* (Kathryn A. Morton Prize; Sarabande, 2005), *Orange Crush* (Sarabande, 2010) and *Disappearing Address*, co-written with Philip Jenks (BlazeVOX, 2010). Some of her honors include a 2013 NEA Poetry Fellowship, a Yaddo residency, 2011 and 2012 Vermont Studio Center Fellowships, Illinois Arts Council Fellowships, a Lewis Faculty Scholar Award, and the PSA's Bright Lights Big Verse Award. She received her Ph.D from the University of Illinois at Chicago, and is an associate professor at Lewis University where she teaches creative writing and film studies, and serves as chief faculty advisor for *Jet Fuel Review*.